THE WORLD OF OCEAN ANIMALS
CLOWN FISH

by Mari Schuh

pogo

Ideas for Parents and Teachers

Pogo Books let children practice reading informational text while introducing them to nonfiction features such as headings, labels, sidebars, maps, and diagrams, as well as a table of contents, glossary, and index.

Carefully leveled text with a strong photo match offers early fluent readers the support they need to succeed.

Before Reading

- "Walk" through the book and point out the various nonfiction features. Ask the student what purpose each feature serves.
- Look at the glossary together. Read and discuss the words.

Read the Book

- Have the child read the book independently.
- Invite him or her to list questions that arise from reading.

After Reading

- Discuss the child's questions. Talk about how he or she might find answers to those questions.
- Prompt the child to think more. Ask: Clown fish live among sea anemones. How do both animals help each other?

Pogo Books are published by Jump!
5357 Penn Avenue South
Minneapolis, MN 55419
www.jumplibrary.com

Library of Congress Cataloging-in-Publication Data

Names: Schuh, Mari C., 1975- author.
Title: Clown fish / by Mari Schuh.
Description: Minneapolis, MN: Jump!, Inc., [2024]
Series: The world of ocean animals | Includes index.
Audience: Ages 7-10
Identifiers: LCCN 2023007485 (print)
LCCN 2023007486 (ebook)
ISBN 9798885245623 (hardcover)
ISBN 9798885245630 (paperback)
ISBN 9798885245647 (ebook)
Subjects: LCSH: Anemonefishes–Juvenile literature.
Classification: LCC QL638.P77 S465 2024 (print)
LCC QL638.P77 (ebook)
DDC 597/.72–dc23/eng/20230323
LC record available at https://lccn.loc.gov/2023007485
LC ebook record available at https://lccn.loc.gov/2023007486

Editor: Jenna Gleisner
Designer: Molly Ballanger

Photo Credits: Sara Nadeea/Shutterstock, cover; 101cats/iStock, 1; Greens and Blues/Shutterstock, 3; Richard Whitcombe/Shutterstock, 4; LeventKonuk/iStock, 5; Kurit afshen/Shutterstock, 6-7; zaferkizilkaya/Shutterstock, 8-9; Rich Carey/Shutterstock, 10; richcarey/iStock, 11; Natural Visions/Alamy, 12-13; Placebo365/iStock, 14-15; Dave Fleetham/Pacific Stock - Design Pics/SuperStock, 16; Ethan Daniels/Shutterstock, 17; ANDREI SAVIN/Alamy, 18-19; Images & Stories/Alamy, 20-21; Kletr/Shutterstock, 23.

Printed in the United States of America at Corporate Graphics in North Mankato, Minnesota.

TABLE OF CONTENTS

CHAPTER 1

BRIGHT FISH

A small fish swims near a **coral reef**. It looks for **algae** and **plankton** to eat. The fish is bright and colorful. It is a clown fish!

Clown fish have bold colors. They can be yellow, orange, or red. Some are a mix of purple and brown. Most have bright white stripes. Some people think their colors look like a clown's face paint. That is how they got their name!

stripe

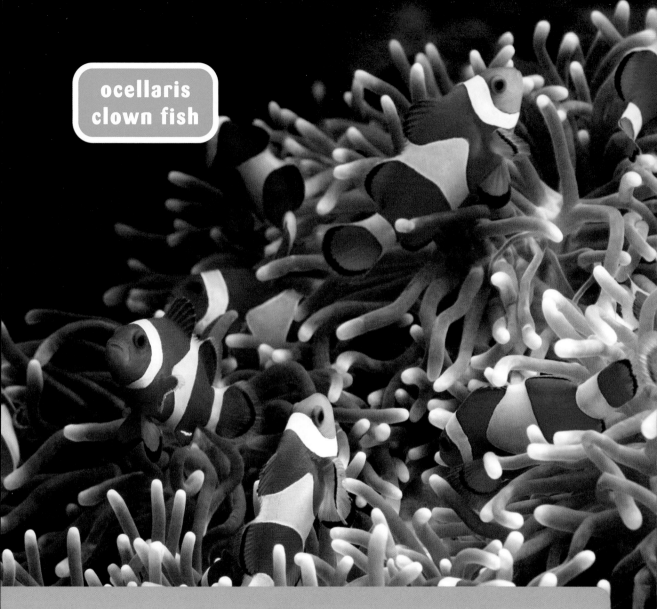

ocellaris
clown fish

Most clown fish live in the Pacific or Indian Ocean. They swim in warm, **shallow** water. Clown fish make their homes in coral reefs. There are at least 30 known **species**. The ocellaris is one of the most well-known.

TAKE A LOOK!

Where do ocellaris clown fish live? Take a look!

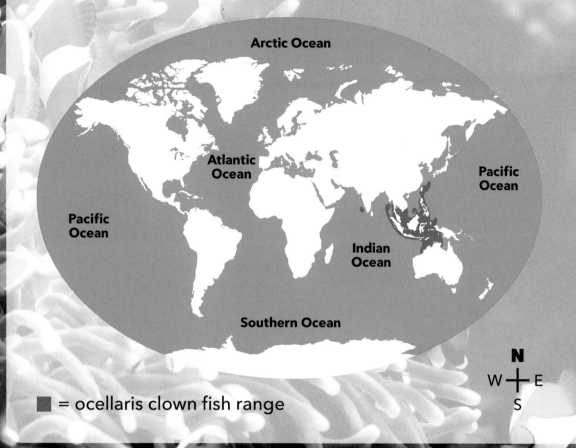

Arctic Ocean

Atlantic Ocean

Pacific Ocean

Pacific Ocean

Indian Ocean

Southern Ocean

N
W — E
S

■ = ocellaris clown fish range

Clown fish are small. Some are only two inches (5.1 centimeters) long. Others grow to be four inches (10 cm).

A clown fish's tail fin is round. This shape does not glide through the water easily. Because of this, clown fish are not strong swimmers.

TAKE A LOOK!

What are the parts of a clown fish? Take a look!

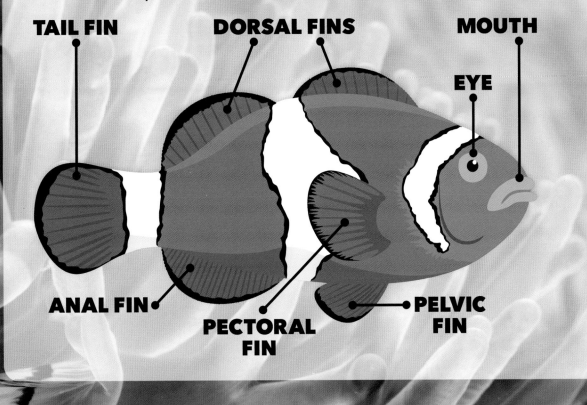

TAIL FIN

DORSAL FINS

MOUTH

EYE

ANAL FIN

PECTORAL FIN

PELVIC FIN

CHAPTER 2

SEA FRIENDS

Clown fish live among sea anemones. These animals have long **tentacles** that sting **prey** with poison. But the tentacles don't hurt clown fish. Why not? Thick **mucus** covers their bodies. This protects the fish from the poison.

tentacle

lionfish

Anemones sting animals that try to eat clown fish. **Predators** such as eels and lionfish stay away.

shrimp

Clown fish help anemones, too. How? They scare away predators that try to eat anemones.

Clown fish also **attract** hungry crabs and shrimp. When they come near, the anemone can sting and eat them.

Clown fish and sea anemones eat each other's food scraps. Clown fish also eat **parasites** off anemones.

DID YOU KNOW?

Clown fish poop is helpful. How? **Nutrients** in it help anemones grow and **reproduce**.

CHAPTER 3

YOUNG CLOWN FISH

Clown fish start life as tiny eggs. Females lay eggs many times a year. They can lay up to 1,000 at a time!

eggs

Some clown fish nests are among anemones' tentacles. Others are on rocks covered by anemones. First, the male clown fish cleans the nest. Then, the female lays her eggs. The male follows closely behind her. He **fertilizes** the eggs.

Clown fish protect their eggs as their young grow. The male moves his fins to fan the eggs. This gives them **oxygen** and keeps them clean. After about one week, the eggs hatch.

DID YOU KNOW?

Clown fish eggs only hatch at night. Why? It is safer. It is harder for predators to see the young clown fish in the dark.

eggs

The tiny, clear **larvae** live on their own. For about two weeks, they float near the ocean's surface as they grow.

They change to look like small adult clown fish. They swim to a coral reef. Each young clown fish will find a sea anemone to call home.

ACTIVITIES & TOOLS

MAKE YOUR OWN MUCUS

Clown fish are covered in thick mucus. Make your own mucus with this fun activity!

What You Need:
- measuring cups and spoons
- glue
- glass bowl
- warm water
- food coloring
- borax
- plastic container

1. **Squeeze about ½ cup (118 milliliters) of glue into a glass bowl.**

2. **Mix in ½ cup (118 mL) of warm water.**

3. **Add a few drops of food coloring.**

4. **Have an adult mix 1 teaspoon (5 mL) of borax into a ½ cup (118 mL) of water in a plastic container and then slowly add the solution to the glue mixture.**

5. **Stir the mixture in one direction until it thickens.**

6. **Knead the slime with your hands until it holds together.**

Thick mucus covers clown fish. It helps them stay safe as they live among sea anemones' tentacles. Feel the mucus you made. What does it feel like? Describe its texture. Can you see how mucus helps a clown fish?

GLOSSARY

algae: Small plants without roots or stems that grow mainly in water.

attract: To gain something's interest.

coral reef: A long line of coral that lies in warm, shallow water.

fertilizes: Begins reproduction by joining sperm cells to egg cells.

larvae: The stage of life clown fish are in right after hatching from their eggs.

mucus: A thick, slimy liquid.

nutrients: Substances needed by people, plants, and animals to stay healthy.

oxygen: A colorless gas found in air and water. Humans and animals need oxygen to breathe.

parasites: Animals or plants that live on or inside another animal or plant.

plankton: Tiny animals and plants that float in oceans and lakes.

predators: Animals that hunt other animals for food.

prey: Animals that are hunted by other animals for food.

reproduce: To produce offspring.

shallow: Not deep.

species: One of the groups into which similar animals and plants are divided.

tentacles: The flexible limbs of some ocean animals.

INDEX

TO LEARN MORE

Finding more information is as easy as 1, 2, 3.

1 **Go to www.factsurfer.com**

2 **Enter "clownfish" into the search box.**

3 **Choose your book to see a list of websites.**

FACT SURFER